Bedtime Prophet Muhammad ﷺ Stories

Saniyasnain Khan

This book is dedicated to my brother, Dr. Zafarul Islam Khan.

Previously published under the title of *The Prophet Muhammad ﷺ Storybook 2*.

First published 2014
Reprinted 2019

Research: Mohammad Zakwan Nadwi
Illustrated by Gurmeet

Goodword Books
1, Nizamuddin West Market, New Delhi-110013
Tel. +9111-41827083, Mob. +91-8588822672
email: info@goodwordbooks.com
www.goodwordbooks.com

Printed in India

Contents

The Marriage of the Prophet

The Prophet Muhammad ﷺ had been used to working for his living since his early youth. By the time he was 25 years old, he was already well known as an honest and hard-working person. Impressed by these qualities, Khadija bint Khuwaylid, a wealthy widow of Makkah, hired him to lead her caravan to Syria and sell her goods in the Syrian markets.

The Prophet Muhammad ﷺ had already made a journey to Syria once earlier with his uncle and he knew the route. He organized the caravan carrying the goods entrusted to him by Khadija very well and once in Syria, conducted the business with great foresight and wisdom, making a fortune for Khadija.

When the Prophet Muhammad ﷺ returned to Makkah, Khadija was very pleased with the way he had conducted his business in Syria and could not believe that he had made so much money for her. She was extremely impressed by his truthful ways and his honest dealings. His persona and pleasing personality made a favorable impression on her and she said to herself:

"I have never met anybody more honest and more trustworthy than Abu Talib's nephew."

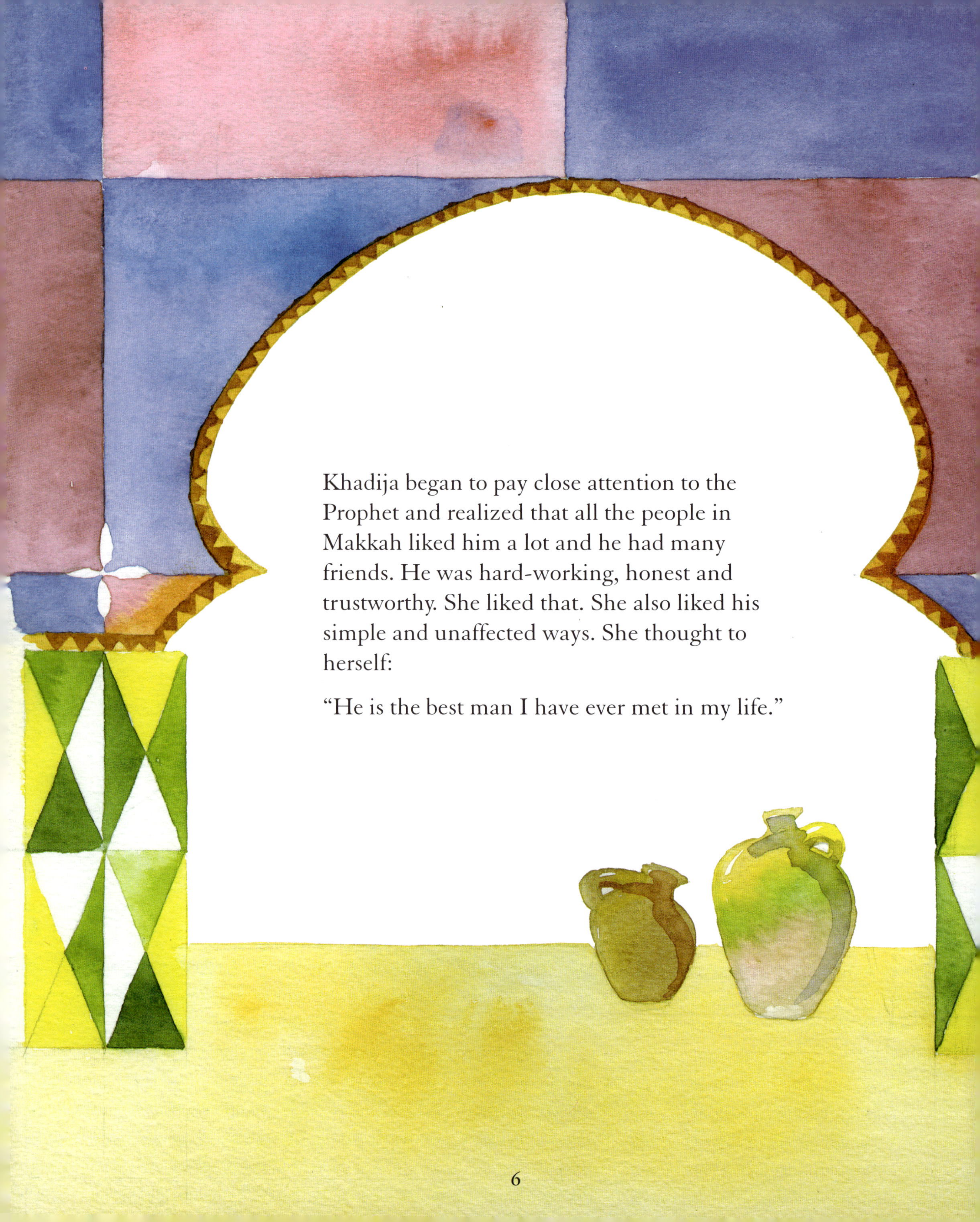

Khadija began to pay close attention to the Prophet and realized that all the people in Makkah liked him a lot and he had many friends. He was hard-working, honest and trustworthy. She liked that. She also liked his simple and unaffected ways. She thought to herself:

"He is the best man I have ever met in my life."

One day one of her best friends, Nafisa bint Munya, came to meet her. They sat together and talked. Then the conversation turned to Khadija's last business venture, the Syrian caravan and the goods it had brought. Khadija remarked:

"I have never made so much money in any of my earlier ventures. I think I was very lucky to have hired Abu Talib's nephew. He managed to sell my goods in Syria for a very good price and whatever he bought with that money and brought to Makkah fetched me a handsome profit as well. He has good business sense and on top of that he is a good and sensible man."

Her friend agreed with her and said:

"Yes, you were very lucky indeed."

And then a sudden thought struck her:

"He is a young man of marriageable age and you are a widow. You are well suited to each other. Why don't you marry him? I can act as the go-between."

Khadija thought for a while and agreed with her:

"You are right. It is a good idea. Help me with this and go and talk to him."

Nafisa went straight to the Prophet Muhammad ﷺ and asked him:

"Why don't you get married?"

He answered truthfully:

"I don't have money to get married. I cannot support a family as yet."

But Nafisa would not give up. She asked:
"What if you are let off from taking on such a responsibility?"

"How could that be possible?" asked the Prophet, wondering what she could mean.

"That is simple and easy. Khadija would like to marry you," explained Nafisa.

This was a pleasant surprise for the Prophet. He had great regard for Khadija and held her in high esteem. He liked the idea of marrying her and promised Nafisa: "I will talk to my uncle and let you know what he thinks."

Abu Talib, the Prophet's uncle, was very pleased when he heard of the marriage proposal. With great joy he immediately agreed to it. The Prophet was happy, too, and in no time the day for the marriage ceremony was fixed.

The marriage became a good occasion for the family and friends to get together. In the presence of the family, Abu Talib read the *nikah* himself. Khadija's father was dead, so her uncle, Amr ibn Asad, was there instead as was her learned cousin, Waraqah ibn Nawfal. The Prophet's foster mother, Halima Sadia, was there too.

For a few days after the *nikah* the Prophet and Khadija lived at the house of Abu Talib. Then Khadija bought a house from her nephew, Hakim ibn Hizam, and they moved there.

The Prophet's Family

The new house into which the Prophet Muhammad ﷺ and Khadija moved was very nice, though not very big. But it had enough space for everybody. It even had a little walled courtyard behind the house where they could sit after sunset.

The Prophet Muhammad ﷺ and Khadija did not live by themselves in their new house. There were many more people who lived with them. First of all, there was Umm Ayman, the old maid of Amina, the Prophet's mother, who had brought him up after his mother died. The Prophet was very fond of her because she reminded him of his childhood and his mother.

Then there was Zayd ibn Haritha, a slave whom Khadija gave to her husband to help him with his work. But the Prophet, who was very kind and disliked any sort of oppression, immediately freed Zayd ibn Haritha and treated him like his own son. Zayd ibn Haritha loved the Prophet so much that when his own family came to take him back home, he refused to go with them because he did not want to be parted from the Prophet. He stayed on with the Prophet for many years to come.

Later on, when his own father died, Zubayr ibn Awwam also came to stay with the Prophet and Khadija and became one of the first people to accept Islam.

The Prophet and Khadija had six children, two boys and four girls. Unfortunately, both the boys, Qasim and Abdullah, died when they were still little babies.

The four daughters: Zaynab, Ruqayya, Umm Kulthum and Fatima, grew up into beautiful young girls and were married when the time came.

Zaynab was married to Khadija's nephew, Abu al-As ibn Rabia, the son of Khadija's sister. He was a kind and upright man and they were very happy together.

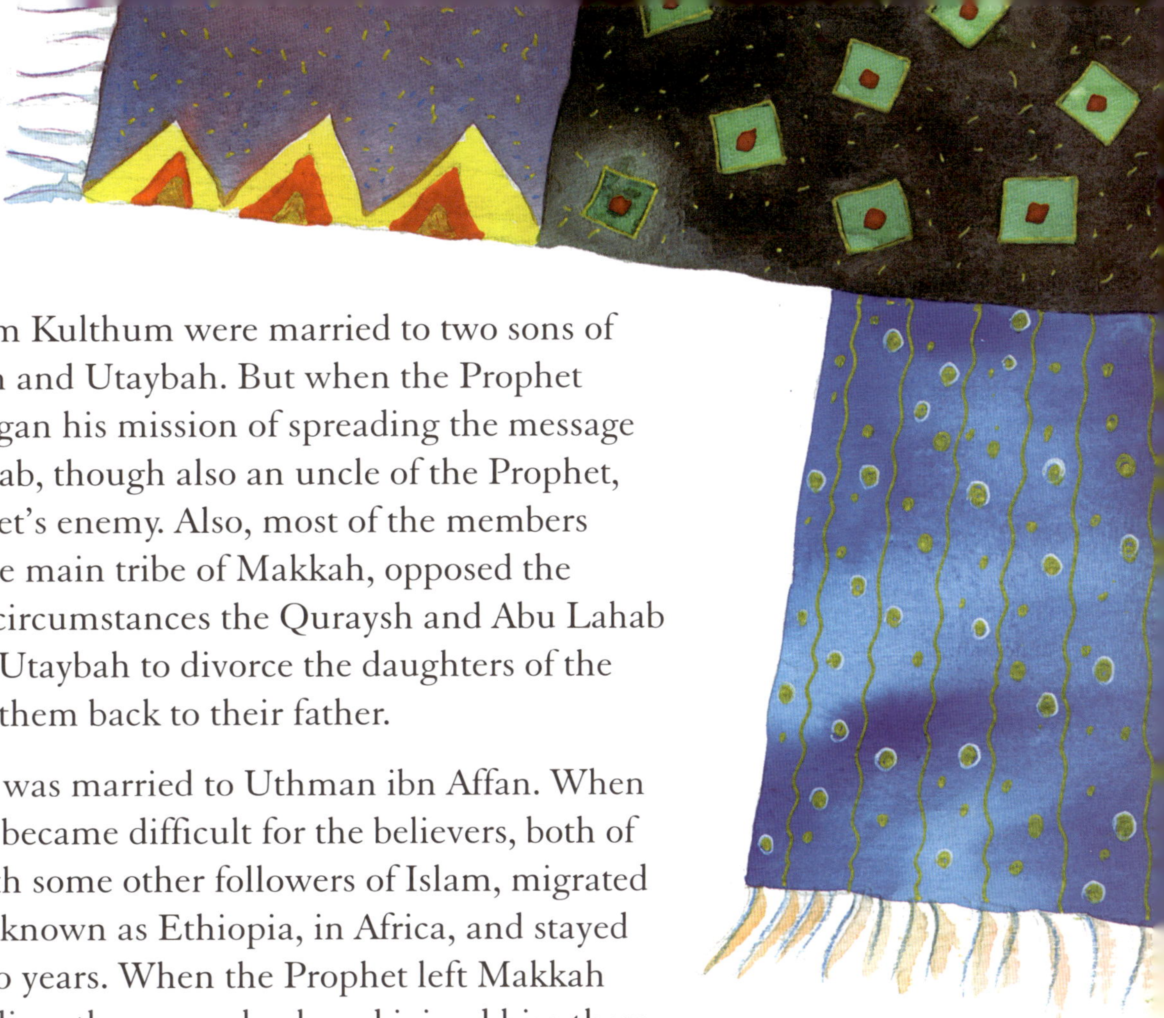

Ruqayya and Umm Kulthum were married to two sons of Abu Lahab, Utbah and Utaybah. But when the Prophet Muhammad ﷺ began his mission of spreading the message of Islam, Abu Lahab, though also an uncle of the Prophet, became the Prophet's enemy. Also, most of the members of the Quraysh, the main tribe of Makkah, opposed the Prophet. In these circumstances the Quraysh and Abu Lahab forced Utbah and Utaybah to divorce the daughters of the Prophet and send them back to their father.

Later on Ruqayya was married to Uthman ibn Affan. When things in Makkah became difficult for the believers, both of them, together with some other followers of Islam, migrated to Abyssinia, now known as Ethiopia, in Africa, and stayed there for about two years. When the Prophet left Makkah and settled in Madina, they came back and joined him there. Some time before the battle of Badr, Ruqayya fell sick and died soon after. After her death, the Prophet married his other daughter, Umm Kulthum, to Uthman ibn Affan, but she too did not live long.

The youngest daughter, Fatima, married her father's cousin and son of Abu Talib, Ali. They had two sons, Hasan and Husain. The Prophet loved his grandsons very much and playing with them gave the Prophet a lot of joy.

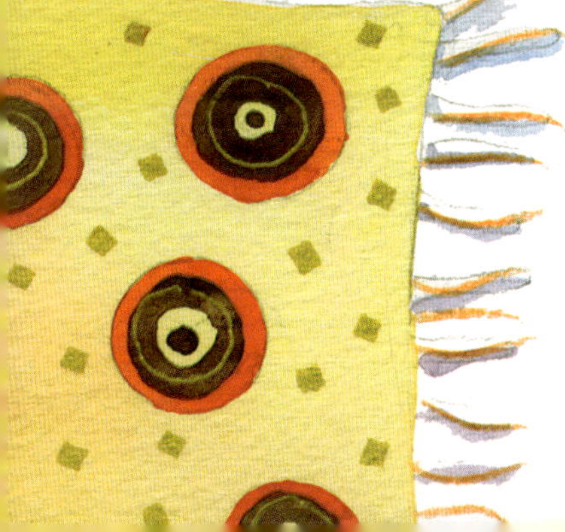

Thinking Deeply About the Creator

Marriage with Khadijah gave the Prophet an opportunity to lead a comfortable life as a wealthy and respected noble of Makkah. And, indeed, for a few years the Prophet Muhammad ﷺ led an uneventful and quiet life of a merchant. However, though busy with his business activities, the Prophet always found time to think about things other than what everyday life brought in its daily routine. Finally, a time came when he gave up all worldly activities and set out to search for the truth.

Since his early years the Prophet liked to spend time alone and try to answer the questions coming to his mind: "Who has made this world? Why are people born and why do they die? What is the meaning of their lives? And how to reach the ultimate Truth?"

The Prophet knew that these questions had answers. But the answers could not be found in the bustle of daily life. So he began to take time off from his everyday pursuits. Instead of meeting people all the time in their homes and at gatherings, and trying to gain for himself a position among the nobles of Makkah, the Prophet Muhammad ﷺ would wander into the barren hills of the desert. He would sit for hours in the wilderness and ponder upon the mysteries of creation. The vast silence of the desert, with its seemingly endless sand and clear sky and at night, equally endless darkness, alive only with the twinkling of millions and millions of tiny stars, seemed to bring one very close to the Creator.

Often the Prophet Muhammad ﷺ would climb up the mountain called Jabal al-Nur, or the Mountain of Light, three miles away from Makkah. Near the top of this mountain there was a cave called the Cave of Hira. This was his favorite retreat and he loved to sit there and contemplate the view in front of him.

When the night came, the Prophet would look at the sky sparkling with stars and would be filled with wonder at its grandeur. He could spend many days in this manner, coming back home only to get more food and water. There was nothing he loved more than the solitude of nature to pray and meditate in, asking the Maker of the heavens and earth for the answers to all the questions that surged in his mind: "What is man's true role in life? What does the Lord require of us, His servants?"

In the year 610 A.D., the Prophet Muhammad ﷺ, now forty years of age, went as was his habit to the Cave of Hira to spend Ramadan, the traditional month of retreat. He was sitting all alone in this cave, when he had an extraordinary experience.

The Angel Appears in the Cave

One day, after many days of the Prophet's meditation, the Archangel Jibril, or Gabriel, suddenly appeared before the Prophet Muhammad ﷺ in human form.

"Read!" commanded the angel.

"I cannot read," the Prophet Muhammad ﷺ protested.

So the angel held the Prophet Muhammad ﷺ tightly by the shoulders, shook him, and taught him these words:

Read: In the name of your Lord who created, created man from a clot.

Read: And your Lord is the Most Generous

who taught by the pen, taught man what he did not know.

These were the first words of the Revelation. The Prophet Muhammad ﷺ felt that these lines were actually being written in his heart.

But the experience left him surprised and confused. He even felt he might be falling ill. Gradually, the Prophet Muhammad ﷺ began to understand—his quest for truth has finally been rewarded. His restless, searching soul has been joined with his Lord.

Allah not only gave him guidance, but He also chose the Prophet Muhammad ﷺ as His Prophet and special Messenger, to bring His word to a world that had gone badly astray. It was a tremendous responsibility. But the Prophet Muhammad ﷺ, far from becoming vain or proud, remained as good and humble a man as ever.

The Prophet Muhammad ﷺ continued to receive divine revelations from time to time over the next twenty-three years. The Archangel Jibril would come to him in different forms, sometimes huge and filling the horizon, and sometimes just a pair of eyes watching him. Sometimes he remained invisible. Occasionally only his voice could be heard. Sometimes the voice was muffled, like a ringing in the Prophet Muhammad's head. But the meaning was always clear.

The Prophet Muhammad ﷺ could neither make the revelations happen, nor could he stop them. They could descend on him at any time. They used

to happen while he was making a speech, while sitting, while praying, or even while riding his camel. He always knew when they were about to take place and his Companions could see the change come over him. He would become silent and normally would lie down wrapped up in his cloak. His face might become red and he would perspire profusely, even on cold days. His Companions said that if one were near him, one could hear something like humming around his face.

The experience of the revelations always seemed to make the Prophet Muhammad ﷺ feel close to death, as if he was leaving his body and might never return.

"Not once did I receive a revelation without thinking that my soul had been torn away," said the Prophet.

At the end of the experience, the Prophet Muhammad ﷺ would return to normal and recite the newly revealed verses of the Quran. His Companions were instructed to memorize them and record them.

The Meeting with Waraqah ibn Nawfal

The experience in the Cave of Hira shook the Prophet to his core. He did not know what to make of it. Disturbed and frightened, he went straight home and told Khadija about the incident. He said:

"Khadija, I do not understand what has happened to me. I fear for my life."

Seeing him trembling in shock and distress, Khadija put a blanket over him and comforted him, saying:

"Allah will never let you down. You are kind to your family. You are truthful. You help the needy and the poor. You gladly welcome anybody who comes as a guest to your house. You follow the way of truth and justice. There is nothing for you to fear."

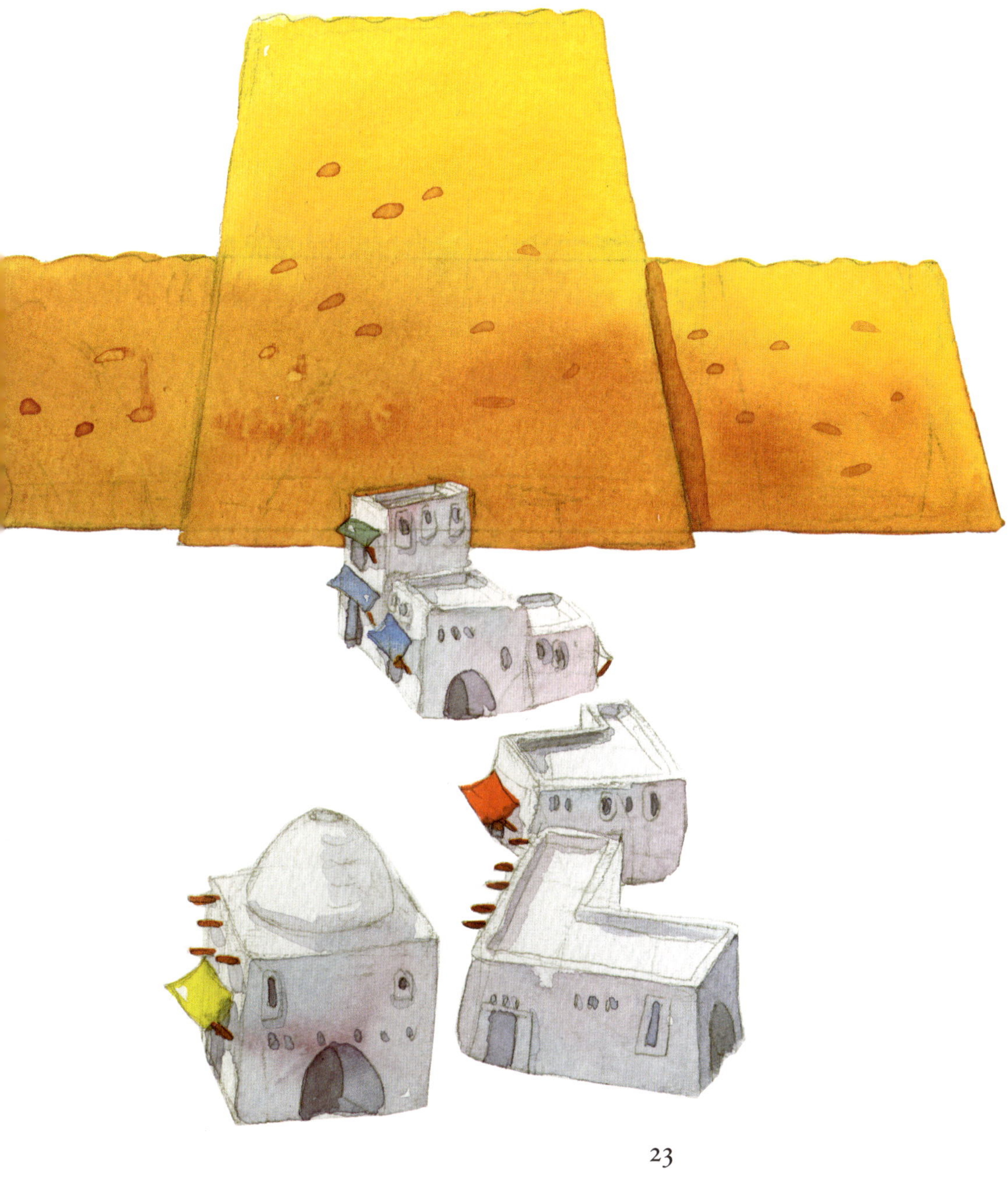

When the Prophet finally fell asleep, Khadija hurried straight to Waraqah ibn Nawfal, her cousin, for advice. Waraqah was a very learned and spiritual man and Khadija trusted his judgment. She told him about what had happened in the cave of Hira and wanted to know what he thought of it all. Having heard her account, Waraqah said:

"If what you say is true, there is no doubt, this must have been the very same angel that visited the Prophets Musa عليه السلام and Isa عليه السلام."

Later on, Khadija took the Prophet to meet Waraqah. The Prophet told him of his experience in the cave. After listening to his words, Waraqah said:

"You will be the Prophet to this nation."

He promised that if he were still alive, he would help in the mission of the Prophet. But Waraqah, being an old, blind man, passed away soon after.

The Angel Teaches How to Say Prayer

Gradually, the Prophet began to understand the meaning of the revelation. At the same time, he realized that a great responsibility of spreading the message of the Quran to all people had fallen on his shoulders.

It was the year 610 AD. The Prophet Muhammad ﷺ was then 40 years old and he and Khadija had been married for 15 years.

At first the mission of spreading Islam was confined to his close relatives. Only later on did Allah command the Prophet to take the message to people at large.

Khadija was the first person to accept Islam. She took no time acknowledging the Prophet and believing in him. She had always known him to be trustworthy and truthful.

One day, the angel Jibril came to the Prophet and taught him how to perform the ablution (*wudu*). He then taught the Prophet how to say the prayer (*salah*). To make sure that he remembered all the movements and words properly, the Prophet said his prayers for the first time alongside the angel Jibril. Later on the Prophet went home and taught *wudu* and *salah* to Khadija. Thereafter, accompanied by Khadija, the Prophet started to pray in his own house.

One day, his cousin, Ali ibn Abi Talib, who was just ten years old, visited their house as usual and saw the Prophet and Khadija praying together. He was surprised and asked:

"What is this? I have never seen anybody doing this before."

The Prophet explained to his little cousin:

"We are saying prayers, or *salah*. Allah has made me His Prophet and revealed the Quran to me. Why don't you join us?"

Ali took in the words and decided to think over the whole matter. The next day he came again to their house and said:

"I want to join you. I accept Islam and want to follow its teachings."

Thus Ali became the second believer after Khadija.

From that time on, the Prophet would lead the prayers and Ali would stand next to him with Khadija standing behind them. They were the only three people offering *salah*. At that time only two prayers, *Fajr* and *Isha*, each with two rak'ahs, were prescribed.

A few days after receiving the first revelation of the Quran, the Prophet received the second revelation. It was the beginning of chapter 74, *al-Muddaththir.* It commanded the Prophet to call people to God and tell them of the creation plan of the Creator.

The Prophet knew what was expected of him and immediately planned to work for *dawah*. His wife, Khadija, and his cousin, Ali ibn Abi Talib, had already accepted Islam. Then there was Zayd ibn Haritha, a former slave whom Khadija had gifted to the Prophet. Zayd ibn Haritha also lived with the Prophet and assisted him in his work. The Prophet treated him as his own son. When the Prophet invited Zayd to accept Islam, Zayd lost no time in entering the fold of Islam. Afterwards the Prophet explained the message of Islam to his four daughters, Zaynab, Umm Kulthum, Ruqayyah and Fatima. They too immediately accepted Islam. In this way, the Prophet's entire family came into the fold of Islam.

All these people would read whatever portion of the Quran was revealed, and would pray to Allah as taught by the Prophet. Also, they would together plan to do *dawah* among the citizens of Makkah.

Abu Bakr Accepts Islam

One day, Abu Bakr ibn Abi Quhafa left his house and went to meet his childhood friend, the Prophet Muhammad ﷺ.

When Abu Bakr came to the Prophet, he said, "O Abul Qasim, these days I don't see you in the meetings of the Makkan people. People blame you for having abandoned our deities. Also I heard that you believe our forefathers and elders were fools and misguided."

The Prophet answered, "Yes, it is true. I am the Prophet of God, and I invite you to believe in one God and I call you to be obedient to Him."

He further added, "By God, this is the truth. You should not associate anyone as an equal to Allah and should worship Him alone."

After that the Prophet recited some verses of the Quran.

Abu Bakr was overwhelmed with emotion. He immediately testified to the authenticity of the Prophet Muhammad's prophethood and accepted Islam.

The Prophet became so happy when Abu Bakr embraced Islam, that there was no one as happy as he was in the whole of Makkah.

Even after many years, the Prophet would often say, "Everyone whom I had invited to Islam was filled with some kind of hesitation but Abu Bakr accepted my message at once and without any doubt."

It was for this quality that Abu Bakr was known as Siddiq, "the one who testifies to the truth".

After accepting Islam, Abu Bakr asked the Prophet, "Now, tell me, what is my work to be?"

The Prophet replied, "The same work for which I have been sent forth." Meaning, calling people to God or doing *dawah* work.

Abu Bakr was a very gentle, kind and noble man, therefore he was well liked by the people. He had a good knowledge of history and genealogy – knowledge of the families

and their forefathers – and was greatly admired for his good memory and wisdom. Also, because he was a tradesman, many people knew him well.

Abu Bakr was already 36 years old at that time, so he planned to do *dawah* work in an organized manner. He started *dawah* work among the people he knew and, due to his efforts, a number of people accepted Islam. Some of the notable names and the age of each person at that time is given below:

Uthman ibn Affan – 34 years old,

Abdul Rahman ibn Awf – 30 years old,

Sa‘d ibn Abi Waqqas – 27 years old,

Zubayr ibn al-Awwam – 22 years old,

Talha ibn Ubaydullah – 13 years old.

Abu Bakr brought these people to meet the Prophet. They all accepted Islam and joined the mission of the Prophet, giving it much strength in the early period. Under the guidance of the Prophet and Abu Bakr, these people began to spread the teachings of Islam in Makkah. As a result of their efforts, many more people entered the fold of Islam. Some of the names are as follows:

Abu Ubaydah ibn al-Jarrah,

Ubaydah ibn Harith ibn Abdul Muttalib,

Uthman ibn Maz‘un,

Arqam ibn Abi al-Arqam,

Fatimah bint al-Khattab (sister of Umar ibn Khattab),

Sa'id ibn Zayd,
Aisha bint Abu Bakr,
Asma bint Abu Bakr and
Khabbah ibn Arat.

After some time, yet another group of people entered the fold of Islam due to the *dawah* work of those who had already accepted Islam. Some of the names of this group are as follows:

Umayr ibn Abi Waqqas,
Abdullah ibn Mas'ud,
Abdullah ibn Jahsh,
Ja'far ibn Abi Talib and his wife Asma,
Khalid ibn Sa'id ibn al-'As,
'Ammar ibn Yasir and
Bilal ibn Rabah al-Habashi.

With this the total number of Muslims in Makkah rose to 40. This included men, women and children. Now, Islam had come into the limelight in Makkah and people were beginning to talk about it a lot.

The First Dawah Centre

Arqam ibn al-Arqam, a sixteen-year-old youth, who had recently accepted Islam, lived near the Safa hillock. His house was a bit isolated and there were no neighbours looking to see who came there. It was therefore easy for the Companions to come there whenever they wanted.

This house became the first centre in which to carry out *dawah* activities. Here the people would meet and recite whatever portions of the Quran were revealed till that times. The Prophet would personally instruct people to write and commit the Quran to memory. He would also explain to them the verses so that they might understand their meaning. In this way, the house of Arqam, which was known as Dar al-Arqam, became the first training centre of Islam.

As Dar al-Arqam was at a distance from the other houses in Makkah, for a long time the Quraysh had no idea that the Prophet and his Companions gathered there and conducted their meetings.

The only curriculum for the training of the companions in Dar al-Arqam was the Quran, which was incomplete at that point of time, as it was still in the process of being revealed. The Quran was the only literature of the Prophet's mission. It contained the fundamental profession of faith and was the handbook of prayer and worship. It mentioned Paradise, Hell and accountability on the Day of Judgment. In this way, the Quran became the first and only textbook for the training of the Companions and preparing the first team of *da'is* (those who call people to God) to take forward the message of Islam.

This first team of Companions was able to successfully spread the message of Islam in Makkah. Due to their efforts, in almost all the tribes in Makkah there were people who came into the fold of Islam. For example:

Abu Bakr (the tribe of Taym),
Uthman ibn 'Affan (the tribe of Banu Umayyah),
'Ali ibn Abi Talib (the tribe of Banu Hashim),
Zubayr ibn al-'Awwam (the tribe of Banu Asad),
Mus'ab ibn 'Umayr (the tribe of Banu Abd al-Dar),
'Abdul Rahman ibn 'Awf (the tribe of Banu Zuhra),
Sa'id ibn Zayd (the tribe of Banu 'Adi),
Abdullah ibn Mas'ud (the tribe of Huzayl),
Ammar ibn Yasir (the tribe of 'Ans), and
Tufayl ibn 'Amr (the tribe of Daws).

In this way, the *dawah* work in Makkah began to take on a good shape. Meanwhile, the Quraysh had discovered that more and more people were following the Prophet. They were not happy with the mission of the Prophet, which was taking people away from their old tribal ways and they tried to stop it by creating obstacles and difficulties.

Early Preaching

Once a year, during the period of Hajj, many people from all over Arabia would gather for the pilgrimage to Makkah. The Prophet Muhammad ﷺ would use this opportunity to meet people in their gatherings and present Islam to them. He would read out portions of the Quran to enlighten them.

In the same way, the Prophet would go to the various fairs, such as Ukaz, Majnnah and Dhul Majaz. A lot of people came to the fairs to trade camels and everyday goods. Therefore, these were good occasions to meet more and more people and tell them about Islam.

Abdullah ibn Wabisah al-Abasi recounts that his father and grandfather were in Mina during the Hajj. The Prophet Muhammad ﷺ came to meet them in their tents.

This is what Abdullah ibn Wabisah al-Abasi had to say about the first meeting with the Prophet in his own words:

“We were staying near Khaif at the first stoning pillar when the Prophet came. He was mounted on his she-camel. Zayd ibn Haritha was sitting right behind him. The Prophet presented Islam to us and called us to accept Islam. None of us said a word in response to his call. The Prophet kept on preaching and we all stood listening to him without responding to him at all.

"Maysara ibn Masruq al-Abasi was also present among us. He was moved by the words of the Prophet. He said, "What the Prophet is saying makes a lot of sense to me. It would be great if we took him into the midst of our caravan."

His people answered, "Don't do this. No one is going to listen him."

When the Prophet heard the good and encouraging words, he said to Maysara, "Why don't you accept it?"

"There is no doubt, what you say sounds very good to me." Maysara replied, "But what can I do? If I accept your religion, my tribe will turn against me. A man can only live with his tribe."

Most of the people were thus set in their old ways and were scared to do without the backing of their own tribes. In this way, no one paid any heed to the Prophet's call, and he returned from there disappointed.

The Prophet Calls from the Hill of Safa

One day, it so happened that the Prophet Muhammad ﷺ decided that the time had come to address the people in an open gathering. He stood atop the little hillock of Safa, near the Kabah, and spoke to the crowd gathered there.

It was an old tradition that if a person had something to announce, he would climb the hill of Safa and speak from there. A crowd would soon gather to hear to what he had to say.

In the same way, when the Prophet Muhammad ﷺ stood atop the hillock of Safa, a large crowd gathered to listen to him as he called out loudly, "*Ya Sabaha.*"

He then asked, "O people of the Quraysh, if I told you that an army was advancing to attack you from the nearby hills, would you believe me?"

"Yes, we would surely believe you," answered the people, "We have always known you to be truthful."

Having heard their answer, the Prophet then called the different tribes by their name.

"O Banu Abdul Muttalib! O Banu Abd Manaf! O Banu Zuhrah! The way you sleep, you will die. The way you get up from sleep you will be raised again after death. After that, either there is eternal paradise or eternal hell."

People remained silent on hearing these words.

The Prophet went on and told them, "Allah has made me the Last Prophet to mankind

and revealed the Quran to me. We must worship one God and submit ourselves to His will. If you will not do so, you will be accountable on the Day of Judgement, and God will punish you."

Abu Lahab, who was one of the uncles of the Prophet, was also present among the crowd. He shouted in derision, "Was this all you called us here for?"

Then he said to the gathering, "Do not listen to a word of that he says. Go back to your homes. Muhammad has lost his mind."

The people, who held Abu Lahab in high esteem, as he was an important man in Makkah, started to disperse. After a while, only Ali ibn Abi Talib, who was just ten years old, and Zayd ibn Haritha remained there with the Prophet.

The Beginning of Difficult Times

When the Prophet Muhammad ﷺ began his mission of *dawah* work – conveying the message of the Quran to the people at large. His own tribe, the Quraysh, refused to support him. Rather, they began to mock him. When they saw that this had no effect on the Prophet and that he continued to carry on his work, they started to persecute him in the most terrible ways.

One day it happened that the Prophet was so badly injured by the stones thrown at him by the people of the Quraysh, that by the time he got back home he was bleeding. His family was appalled to see him in this state but he comforted them and said:

"Don't worry, it is nothing. The wounds will heal in no time."

However, the next day, the Prophet was in so much pain, due to the injuries on his face and body, that he could not go to the Kabah to pray. So the handful Muslims who had gathered in the Kabah to pray, performed their prayers without the Prophet. When these people prostrated themselves (*sajdah*), all of a sudden the people of the Quraysh tribe attacked them from behind. Many Muslims were seriously injured.

Praying Secretly

Abu Lahab and his wife were close relatives of the Prophet Muhammad ﷺ. In spite of that, they became his most violent enemies. They would throw stones at the Prophet's house and would incite street urchins to do the same. They would even throw dirt and the carcasses of dead animals at the Prophet's house but the Prophet would bear these insults with great patience.

Abu Lahab's wife, Jamila, went to such great lengths to make the Prophet's life miserable that, she would spread thorns on the path along which the Prophet was to pass. Often sharp thorns would pierce the Prophet's feet, making it impossible for him to walk. When he reached his home, he would painstakingly remove the thorns, and blood would ooze from the wounds all over his feet. This made it difficult for him to walk for many days to come.

Moreover, not a single day passed without the Prophet returning from the Kabah with some part or the other of his body bleeding. The people of the Quraysh would injure him by cruelly throwing stones at him.

Sa'd ibn Abi Waqqas, an early Companion of the Prophet says:

"At that time, it was not possible for us Muslims to perform a congregational prayer at the Kabah. It was only possible to gather at some place other than the Kabah, as the Quraysh constantly kept a watch over us. If we gathered at the house of any Muslim, the Quraysh would immediately get to know about it and would attack us, inflicting serious injuries on us.

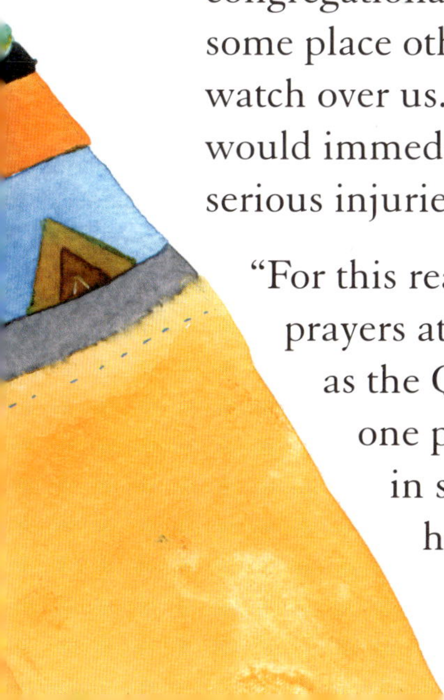

"For this reason, we would go out of Makkah and perform our prayers at some remote place. We kept shifting our place of prayer, as the Quraysh would get to know if we said our prayers at any one place on a regular basis. Even if it was outside Makkah in some remote valley, they would follow us there and harass us."

The Purpose of Life

The essence of the Prophet Muhammad's preaching was to tell people about the purpose of life: to explain the creation plan of the Almighty Allah, when He had created the universe. Also, the Prophet answered such questions as: What is life? What is death? What is the purpose for which man has been sent to earth? How should he conduct himself in this life? How should he live in this world to be successful in the Hereafter?

In the early Makkan period, the Prophet received mostly the shorter chapters of the Quran, which dealt mainly with the Day of Judgement, Doomsday, Paradise and Hell.

The Prophet, therefore, would read out these passages of the Quran to people and then would explain to them that this life had been given to them, so that they could make themselves deserving candidates to enter Paradise.

He would explain that the key to enter Paradise was the purification of the soul – *tazkiyah*. This meant that one should banish from one's heart all kinds of negative feelings such as anger, revenge, violence, intolerance, arrogance and the like, and become completely positive in one's personality. Paradise would thus bc given to those who were able to make themselves completely positive souls.

Turkey
Caucasus
Mountain range
Syria
Mediterranean
Sea
Jerusalem
Ur
Egypt
Madinah
Red Sea
Makkah
Arabia
East Africa

The Reaction of the Quraysh

When the Prophet Muhammad ﷺ started preaching the Oneness of Allah, the people of Makkah understood that he was saying that the religion of polytheism they followed was baseless and wrong. Therefore, they turned against the Prophet. Thus began a period of extreme suffering for the Prophet and the handful of Muslims who followed him.

Once, at the request of Abu Bakr, the Prophet Muhammad ﷺ came to the Kabah. Seeing the Prophet there, a number of Muslims gathered at the Kabah. Abu Bakr stood up and started addressing the gathering. While Abu Bakr was giving his speech, some of the people of the Quraysh lost their temper. They rained blows on the Prophet and the other Muslims with all their might. Utbah ibn Rabia hit Abu Bakr so hard in the face that he started bleeding profusely. The Muslims were surrounded on all sides and could not get away from their persecutors. After a short while the relatives of Abu Bakr arrived there and got him out of the clutches of the Quraysh with great difficulty.

Abu Dharr Ghifari

Abu Dharr Ghifari was living far away from Makkah among the tribe of Ghifar. One day he heard that there was a man in Makkah who declared that he was the Messenger of God and that he received the revelations of the Quran from God.

Abu Dharr Ghifari was curious to know more about this person. He sent his elder brother, Unays Ghifari, to Makkah and asked him to find out the truth about this man who claimed to be the Prophet and said that he received revelations from Allah. He also asked him to listen to the revelations and give him his true opinion about the Prophet and his words.

Unays Ghifari took a camel and rode to Makkah. He met the Prophet Muhammad ﷺ and got a good idea about his teachings and message. Unays later left Makkah and arrived back his home.

Once home, Unays Ghifari went to his brother and told him, that he had met Muhammad ibn Abdullah. He found that in Makkah people called him "a liar", "a magician", "a poet" and "a soothsayer."

However, Unays was an intelligent person. He was a poet as well. So he told his brother,

"But I have heard many storytellers and Muhammad's speech was not like that of a storyteller, nor was what he said poetry. I swear to God, he is a truthful person."

Then Unays added, "I saw him preaching goodness and he stopped people from doing evil. He strongly urged people to have a good moral character."

After hearing the good things his brother had to say about the Prophet Muhammad ﷺ, Abu

Dharr Ghifari became inspired to visit Makkah himself. So he prepared his camel. He took his water bag with drinking water and some food to keep him going on the long journey. Then he set out towards Makkah.

After reaching Makkah he first met Ali ibn Abi Talib, who took him to the Prophet Muhammad ﷺ. Abu Dharr Ghifari met the Prophet Muhammad ﷺ and listened to what he had to say. Since Abu Dharr was a truth seeker, it took him no time to convince himself that the Quran was the word of God. He immediately accepted Islam by reciting the *shahadah*.

After accepting Islam, Abu Dharr Ghifari went to the Kabah. He said his prayers there and openly announced his acceptance of Islam. The people of the Quraysh who were present there did not like this. They started beating him. They tortured him so much that Abu Dharr collapsed and fell to the ground. It was only when Al-Abbas came there that he managed to rescue him from his enemies.

Afterwards, the Prophet Muhammad ﷺ told him to go back to his tribe and introduce Islam to them. Then the Prophet added, "For some time, you should remain there and then when you feel that situation here has improved, you could return to me."

So Abu Dharr Ghifari returned to his clan. The first one to accept Islam was his elder brother, Unays Ghifari. Then both the brothers invited their mother to Islam. She too understood the truth in the teachings of Islam, so she also accepted Islam.

In this way Abu Dharr Ghifari and his family began to do *dawah* work among his tribe and, due to their work, almost half of the Ghifari tribe accepted Islam in a few years' time.

The Prophet Invites His Relatives to a Meal

For almost three years, *dawah* activities were limited to individual meetings and private circles.

Later, there came a revelation of the Quran which commanded the Prophet Muhammad ﷺ to perform *dawah* publicly: "Warn your close relatives."

So the Prophet Muhammad ﷺ invited people of his clan the Banu Hashim for a meal. The charge of organizing the meal was given to Ali ibn Abi Talib, who arranged milk and dates for the guests.

About forty men of the Banu Hashim assembled at the Prophet's house. After they had had their meal, the Prophet gave a brief speech.

He said, "I have come to you as a blessing for the world and the hereafter. I don't know if in all of Arabia anyone has brought a better thing than this. Tell me who will support me."

And then the Prophet added, "Whoever supports me, will be in Paradise with me."

Since the message of Islam had already reached most of the people, it was not difficult to understand what the Prophet said.

There was pin drop silence. No one said a single word. The Prophet repeated his words two or three times. But no one responded to his call.

Seeing this Ali ibn Abi Talib, who was about 12 year old, got up and said,

"Though I have pain in my eyes and my legs are weak, though I am the youngest of you all, O my brother, I will support you."

Seeing this the Prophet exclaimed, "You O Ali, You O Ali!" Meaning, you are merely a young boy, how can you help me and support me.

Also present at the gathering was Al-Abbas, the Prophet's uncle, who was a rich man. He could easily have made himself responsibile for the Prophet and supported him in his cause. But he too remained silent.

All the relatives who were assembled there got up and went away. No one showed any interest in helping or supporting the Prophet in his mission of *dawah* work.

The Sun on the One Hand, the Moon on the Other

The Quraysh wanted to stop the Prophet Muhammad ﷺ from spreading his new religion. They attacked him. They abused him. They tortured his Companions. They even killed some of them. But the Prophet did not react and continued his work with patience, as he had been commanded by Allah to convey the message of the Quran to others.

The Quraysh knew that since Abu Talib, the Prophet's uncle, was protecting him and helping in his work, so they came to meet Abu Talib. They told him to tell his nephew, Muhammad, to stop his activities.

Abu Talib called the Prophet Muhammad ﷺ and asked him to stop his mission as it would be very difficult for him to bear the enmity of the Quraysh.

The Prophet Muhammad ﷺ replied, "O Uncle! By God Almighty, even if they put the sun on my right hand and the moon on my left hand, I will not stop my work."

Seeing the firm commitment and zeal the Prophet showed by saying such fine words, Abu Talib was moved too. "Go forth, my nephew," assured Abu Talib, "and do what you want to do. I swear by God that I will never hand you over to your enemies."

In the tribal age, there were no police, no army and no government as we have today. So no person could survive without the support of his tribe. The Prophet belonged to the Banu Hashim. Due to Abu Talib's support for and protection of the Prophet Muhammad ﷺ, the entire clan of the Banu Hashim came to the support of the Prophet Muhammad ﷺ.

Hamza Accepts Islam

One day the Prophet Muhammad ﷺ was praying on top of a hillock in Makkah. When Abu Jahl saw him praying, he took a stone in his hand and hit the Prophet with it. The Prophet got injured and started bleeding profusely. Seeing this a man rushed to Hamza and said, "O Hamza what has happened to your honour, Abu Jahl has hit your nephew very hard with a stone. Why don't you go and help him?"

Hamza was a very strong man, like a wrestler. He had just returned from a hunting trip. He had a bow in his hand made of iron.

Hearing this, Hamza got up in anger and went straight to Abu Jahl's house. He called him from outside the house. As soon as Abu Jahl came out of his house, Hamza hit Abu Jahl very hard with the iron bow he was carrying in his hand. The blow was so hard that Abu Jahl started bleeding from his head.

Afterwards Hamza came to the Prophet Muhammad ﷺ and told him, "Nephew, I have avenged you."

The Prophet calmly replied, "Uncle, I would have been happier if you had accepted Islam."

Hearing these words of the Prophet, Hamza lost no time in repeating the *shahadah*, and embracing Islam.

When Hamza came back home there were some people who condemned him, saying, "You have left the religion of your forefathers. You have become irreligious." Due to this, Hamza became restless and thought that he had probably done something wrong. He could not sleep the whole night. The next morning he went to the Kabah and prayed to Allah, "O Allah, if the way of Muhammad is the right way, then implant the firmness of truth in my heart. Otherwise let me come out this state in which I find myself now. Open my heart to the truth and let my suspicion vanish."

Later he met the Prophet Muhammad ﷺ and told him what was going on in his heart.

The Prophet clarified his doubts and gave him the good news of Paradise and warned him about Hellfire. After this his heart calmed down and his mind became easy about the truthfulness of the Prophet's message.

Hamza said to the Prophet, "I bear witness that you speak the truth."

"O my nephew," said Hamza, "I am going to announce that I have accepted Islam and will not give it up, even if I were given everything on which the sun rises."

Due to Hamza's accepting Islam, some other people also accepted Islam and the number of Muslims rose to thirty.

Abu Sufyan Meets the Prophet

Once Abu Sufyan was going to his farm on horseback with his wife, Hind. His son Muawiyah, who was still quite young, was riding a donkey. Abu Sufyan saw the Prophet Muhammad ﷺ coming towards them. He told his son, Muawiyah, to get down from the donkey and let the Prophet ride it. Muawiyah got down and let the Prophet mount the donkey. The Prophet rode along with them for a while.

The Prophet then addressed them, saying, "O Sufyan ibn Harb and O Hind bint Utbah, I swear by God, you will surely die one day. You will be raised again after death. Then the righteous will go to Paradise and the wicked will go to Hell."

Muawiyah says that after telling them this, the Prophet got down from the donkey and went away. Then he remounted the donkey.

He says, my mother said to my father, "Was it for this magician that you got my son down from the donkey?" To which Abu Sufyan replied, "I swear by God, he is not a magician, he is not a liar."

Sumayyah, the First Martyr in Islam

Abu Jahl was one of the direst enemies of Islam and the Prophet Muhammad ﷺ. He had a maid whose name was Sumayyah. Abu Jahl had bought her as a slave.

When the teachings of the Prophet Muhammad ﷺ spread in Makkah, Sumayyah also became influenced by them and accepted Islam.

When Abu Jahl came to know about Sumayyah's acceptance of Islam, he became furious. He said to Sumayyah, "You must abandon this new faith." "I will not leave Muhammad's religion," said Sumayyah firmly.

This made Abu Jahl even more furious. He took some ropes and tied her to a pole. He flogged her so much that she fainted.

In those days slaves had no rights. Since Sumayyah was a slave no one could come to her rescue.

When Abu Bakr came to know about it, he decided to meet Abu Jahl and set her free by handing over some money. He had already bought six slaves who had accepted Islam and set them free.

He came to Abu Jahl and offered one hundred dirhams to sell Sumayyah to him, so that he could set her free. Abu Jahl did not agree to this, so he offered one hundred and fifty dirhams. But Abu Jahl did not agree to his offer. Then Abu Bakr said, “Tell me what amount you need, and I will pay it.” But Abu Jahl would not agree to sell Sumayyah at any cost.

Sumayyah worked as a midwife too. So many women of the Quraysh whom Sumayyah had helped in child birth, came and pleaded with Abu Jahl not to torture Sumayyah any more. But he did not listen to anyone. Abu Jahl flogged Sumayyah so much that her entire body was covered with deep wounds and blood started flowing from everywhere. Though she was almost fainting, she kept repeating, “I will not leave Muhammad’s religion.”

At last when Sumayyah would not listen to Abu Jahl, he took her one day near to the Kabah and asked in front of all the people, “Will you leave the religion of Muhammad or not?”

Sumayyah said, “No”, to this. Abu Jahl became red with anger and hit her so hard with the spear in his hands that Sumayyah died on the spot.

Thus Sumayyah became the first martyr of Islam.

Umar ibn Al-Khattab

There were two people in Makkah who were distinguished for their unmatched leadership qualities. They were Umar ibn al-Khattab and Amr ibn Hisham, who was also known as Abu Jahl.

The Prophet Muhammad ﷺ once prayed, “O Allah, give support to Islam through one of these two Umars.” The Prophet’s prayer was answered and after some time Umar ibn al-Khattab embraced Islam.

‘Umar ibn al-Khattab was an important man of Makkah. He was rich. He was very brave. And he was also very stubborn.

‘Umar refused to accept Islam. He troubled the Muslims. He did not let them pray in peace. And he threatened to beat anybody who opposed him. People were very afraid of him.

One day the Prophet and his followers gathered in a house to pray. ‘Umar came to know about it. Sword in hand, he rushed towards the house. A man saw him walking in haste and asked him: “Where are you going with a sword in your hand?” ‘Umar said: “I am going to kill Muhammad. He is spreading mischief among our people.”

The man said to 'Umar: "If you kill Muhammad, his tribe will kill you. Let him be. It would be better if you saw what is happening in your own family." "What is the matter with my family?" asked 'Umar. The man answered: "Your sister and her husband have become Muslims. And you know nothing about it!"

'Umar turned around and ran to his sister's house. He stopped outside the door and listened. He could hear somebody reading aloud. He pushed the door open and went in.

'Umar's sister hid the paper from which they were reading. Seeing this, 'Umar became so angry that he hit his sister. Then he hit his brother-in-law.

He said: "Have you become Muslims?" They were afraid of 'Umar but loved Allah best. They said: "Yes. We are Muslims. We believe in Allah and His Prophet. Do what you like."

When 'Umar saw that he had hurt his sister, he became ashamed. He said to her: "Give me that paper. Let me read what is written there."

She handed him over the paper on which, *Surah Ta Ha* was written. He started reading it.

When he reached verse 14, "I am Allah. There is no deity save Me; so worship Me alone, and say your prayers in My remembrance", he felt as if these verses were addressed to him in person and Allah was talking to him. He immediately decided not to lose any more time in following the truth. He turned to his sister and brother-in-law and said, "I came to you as an enemy of Islam; I go from you as a friend of Islam. I buckled on this sword to slay the Prophet of Islam; I now go to him to offer my allegiance." Fatima and Sa'id called out, *"Allahu Akbar!"* (God is great!)

'Umar turned around and went to meet the Prophet Muhammad ﷺ. He said to him: "O Messenger of Allah, I have come to tell you that I believe in Allah." The Prophet embraced him. Thus Islam was strengthen by 'Umar ibn al-Khattab becoming a Muslim.

Amr ibn Abasa

Amr ibn Abasa was a truth seeker. He was not content with the religion of his forefathers. So one day he came to know about the Prophet Muhammad ﷺ. Riding a she-camel, he reached Makkah and met the Prophet Muhammad ﷺ. He came to know the people of his tribe were against him, and so, the Prophet was doing his work in secret. After searching for a while, he finally reached the place where the Prophet Muhammad ﷺ was staying. Amr ibn Abasa asked, "Who are you?" "I am the Prophet of God," said the Prophet Muhammad ﷺ.

"What is the meaning of Prophet?" asked Amr ibn Abasa. "The Prophet is a person who brings a message from Allah," replied the Prophet.

"Is it true that Allah has sent you?" asked Amr ibn Abasa.

"Yes," said the Prophet

"To worship One God, and not to associate anyone with Him, and to be kind to relatives and kinsmen," continued the Prophet.

"Who are helping you in this work?" asked Amr ibn Abasa.

"A freeman and a slave," said the Prophet Muhammad ﷺ, meaning Abu Bakr and Bilal.

Then Amr ibn Abasa said, "I want to be with you in your mission."

The Prophet said to him that this was not the right time for him to be there and to become a part of this mission. He told him to return to his village and when he heard favourable news about him, then he should come back.

So Amr ibn Abasa accepted Islam and returned to his home.

Zimad Meets the Prophet

Zimad belonged to the tribe of Azdshanoh. Once he came to Makkah on a pilgrimage. At one place he saw Abu Jahl, Utbah ibn Rabia and Umayyah ibn Khalf talking to each other. Zimad also sat with them. Abu Jahl said, "This man (meaning the Prophet Muhammad ﷺ) has brought discord to our groups. He thinks our pious ancestors were all misguided." To this Umayyah said, "He must be a madman."

On hearing this, Zimad thought that probably the Prophet Muhammad ﷺ had been possessed by some evil spirit. Since he used to cure such people who were possessed by evil spirits, he set out to meet him. He searched for him the whole day, but could not find him. The next day he found the Prophet praying at Maqam Ibrahim near the Kabah. When the Prophet had finished his prayers, Zimad approached him and said, "O Muhammad I cure these

things. If you let me do this for you, hopefully, God will give you a cure and good health."

To this the Prophet Muhammad ﷺ did not respond. The Prophet said, "All praise is due to Allah, we seek help from Him alone. To whom Allah shows the right path, no one can misguide him. And to whom He misguides, no one can bring him to the right path."

The Prophet further said, "I bear witness that only Allah is worth worshipping. No one is His partner." The Prophet said this three times.

Zimad was quite mesmerized by these beautiful words from the Prophet. So he thought that he had heard the storytellers, the magicians and the poets, but what the Prophet said he had never heard in his whole life.

The Prophet extended his hands to Zimad. He took his hands right there and then entered the fold of Islam.

Haseen, the Old Man

Haseen was an old man. He was very respected among the Quraysh tribe. One day some of the members of the Quraysh tribe came to him and said, "Please talk to this man (the Prophet Muhammad ﷺ). He offends our deities."

Haseen agreed to do so and accompanied them to meet the Prophet Muhammad ﷺ.

Haseen said, "I have heard that you offend our deities, though your father was a very good man."

The Prophet asked Haseen, "How many deities do you worship?"

To which Haseen said, "Seven deities on the earth and one in heaven."

The Prophet asked, "When you are in distress, to which deity do you call for help?" "To the one in the heaven," said Haseen.

The Prophet asked him again, "When you suffer some loss in your wealth, to whom do you call for help?" "To the one in the heaven," replied Haseen.

The Prophet said to him that the God who listened to his distress is One. But he associated other gods with him.

Haseen thought that he had never spoken to such a person in his whole life.

Afterwards the Prophet Muhammad ﷺ told Haseen, "Accept Islam, you will be successful in the Hereafter."

Haseen said, "What should I say about my family and children?"

Then the Prophet Muhammad ﷺ taught him a beautiful prayer:

"O Allah, I am a seeker of guidance from You. Please correct my affairs, and give me such knowledge as gives me benefit."

Haseen repeated this prayer and accepted the faith before leaving that place.

This is Better Than That for Which We Have Come Here

A delegation of the Khazraj tribe came to Makkah from Madinah. They were visiting Makkah to make some agreement with the Quraysh tribe. One of the members of the delegation was Iyas ibn Mu'adh.

When the Prophet Muhammad ﷺ came to know about this delegation, he went to meet them.

The Prophet sat with them and said, "Should I tell you something better than that for which you have come here?"

"What is that?" they asked.

The Prophet said, "I am the Prophet sent by Allah. Allah has sent me to His servants, so that I may call people to Allah and tell them that they should worship Allah alone, and not associate anyone with Him. Allah has sent down His book to me." Then the Prophet read some verses from the Quran to them.

Iyas ibn Mu'adh was a young man at that time. When he heard the Prophet, he said to his people, "O my people, I swear to God, this is surely better than that for which you have come here."

Hearing these words from Ibn Mu'adh, Anas ibn Rafay took some dust in his hands and threw it in the face of Ibn Mu'adh, and said, "Leave these things, we have come here for some other purpose." Seeing his anger at and disapproval of the Prophet, Ibn Mu'adh became silent.

Later the Prophet Muhammad ﷺ went away and the people in the delegation left Makkah after completing their work.

Soon after reaching Madinah, Ibn Mu'adh fell ill and passed away. One of the people of his tribe, who was present at the time of his death, said, "Ibn Mu'adh was repeating the words, *'La ilaha illallah Allahu Akbar wa Subhan Allah.'*" Meaning there is no deity other than Allah. God is Great and Glory be to God.

The Prophet Visits Several Tribes

In those days of tribal rules, no one could live without the support of his tribe. After the death of the Prophet's uncle, whose name was Abu Talib, the Prophet lost his biggest supporter and helper.

Now the tribe of the Quraysh became more violent and aggressive in torturing the Muslims and making life difficult for the Prophet Muhammad ﷺ.

During the Hajj season, the Prophet Muhamamd ﷺ would visit the fairs of Ukaz, Majannah and Dhul Majaz and also visit people at their homes and present Islam to them. He also asked people to give him their protection, so that he could carry out his prophetic mission. He would tell them that whoever helped him in this task would be rewarded with Paradise.

Not a single tribe agreed to protect the Prophet Muhammad ﷺ or help him. He went to each and every tribe of Arabia one by one, but none of them agreed to help him or protect him.

He went to the tribe of the Banu Amir ibn Sa‘sa‘ah. They treated the Prophet very badly. They turned him away, throwing stones at him.

The Prophet went to see the people of the tribe of Banu Muharib ibn Khasfa. There was an old man who was a hundred years of age.

The Prophet Muhammad ﷺ told him about the Oneness of Allah (*tawheed*) and asked him to take him under his protection, so that he could convey the message of Allah to the people. The old man replied, “Your tribe knows you better. I swear to God that whoever takes you from here to his place, will be the worst man to take home anything from here on the season of Hajj. Therefore, please excuse me.”

Maysarah ibn Masruq, who was among them, said to the people of their tribe, "I swear to God, if we obey this man and take him to our tribe, it will surely be a good thing for us. I swear to God this man's words will dominate that it will reach everywhere."

Hearing Maysarah, the people of his tribe said, "Leave it, why do you say something which none of us is going to accept?"

When the Prophet heard Maysarah, he became hopeful about him. He said to Maysarah, “Why you yourself do not accept this message.” “What you are saying seems very pleasant to me,” said Maysarah, “but if I accept what you say, my tribe will go against me. And you know that no man can live without the support of his tribe.”

Bibliography

A. Guillaume, *The Life of Muhammad: A Translation of Ibn Ishaq's Sirat Rasul Allah*, Oxford University Press, Karachi, 1967.

Ali Muhammad al-Sallabi, *Al-Sirah al-Nabawiyah*, Dar Ibn Kathir, Damascus, 2007.

Dr. Farida Khanam, *The Life of the Prophet Muhammad ﷺ made simple*, Goodword Books, New Delhi, 2013

Ibn Hisham, *al-Sirah al-Nabawiyyah*, Dar al-Qalam, Beirut, 2009.

Ibn Kathir, *Al-Sirah al-Nabawiyyah*, Darul Fikr, Beirut, 1978.

Maulana Shibli Nu'mani, *Sirat-un-Nabi*, Kitab Bhavan, Delhi, 2008.

Maulana Wahiduddin Khan, *The Prophet Muhammad: A Simple Guide*, Goodword Books, New Delhi, 2007.

Maulana Wahiduddin Khan, *Sirat-e-Rasul*, Goodword Books, New Delhi, 2009.

Maulana Wahiduddin Khan, *The Prophet of Peace*, Penguin Books, New Delhi, 2009.

Maulana Wahiduddin Khan, *Muhammad: A Prophet for All Humanity*, Goodword Books, New Delhi, 2011.

Muhammad Husayn Haykal, *Life of Muhammad*, New Crescent Publishing Company, New Delhi, 2009.

Saniyasnain Khan, *Tell Me About the Prophet Muhammad*, Goodword Books, New Delhi, 2008.